The Funny Travel List Texas: Adventures and Unique Outings

A Comical Thrills Journey Through the
Lone Star State — Puns Jokes and More

Chuck Acts

Contents

———

A Special Gift To Our Readers

———

Included in your purchase of this book, we are giving you a fun information book on Texas Slang, Sayings and the History of where they come from. We hope that you like it!

Click on the link below and let us know which email address to deliver it to:

www.funnytravellist.com

Enjoy this book?

Honest reviews of my books are the only thing that helps bring attention of my books to other readers. I don't have the money to throw at advertising. Not yet anyway. So, If you enjoyed this book, I would be grateful if you could spend just 3 minutes leaving a review (It can be as short as you like).

The review button is on the upper left corner of our website. Just scan the code above and look upper left. - Thank you very much.

Facebook Group
WELCOME TO THE GATHERING!

———

If you want to get even more informative insight on Funny Travel Lists, you can always join our Facebook group. Our group includes: Travelers, Boon Dockers, Campers, RV Enthusiast, New Texans and Adventurers. This group was set up to discuss exploring funny and unique places and tell the stories of what we have come across in the US. We are a tight community seeking additional secret adventures while sharing some of our success and failures out on the road. We discuss all types of subjects and many that the general public are unaware! Stop by and see if we have a Funny Travel List book for your state! Be nice and share in the spirit of helping!

The Funny Travel List Group

www.facebook.com/groups/funnytravellist/

Scan the QR code to easily get to the group

Put on Ya'lls Sitting Britches

"Only Texas can turn defeat into a legend, and a song, and a tourist attraction, and a major motion picture"
- Rosemary Kent (Storm, 2020).

Alright, alright, alright…hot on the heels of the last book, *"The Funny Travel List Texas: Eat & Drink - A Comical Food Journey Through The Lone Star State - Puns, Jokes, Food, and More," ya'll* can now incorporate *travelin'* and places to eat together for the ultimate *Texian* experience.

If you're ever feeling homesick while traveling, or just need a good laugh, take a look at this list of Texas funny travel tips. From dodging armadillos on the road to watching out for cow pies, these quirks of life in the Lone Star State are sure to make you chuckle. So if you're planning a trip to Texas, be sure to check out this list first!

This book covers all the adventure destinations, funny places, and sites great for the whole family, and even those must-see places (some hidden away and lesser-known) that the Lone Star state has to offer.

Texas is not only the second-biggest state in the US but one that has the most to offer. *Ev'thang* is big here (after all, our state is bigger than any country in the whole of Europe). *Havin'* said that you could look forward to *visitin'* sites such as:

- The Alamo — So good it got its own movie.

- As many treehouse accommodations as you can visit.

- Museums boasting ev'thang from sculptures, cattle drives, and just plain oddities.

Best of all is that all these sites will leave you *wonton* to visit as each venue and attraction is laced with unique Texiasms to boost *yer* language skills and even a bit of side humor.

The book is *yer* all-encompassing blueprint guide and travel companion to take you to some of Texas' most notable sites for an authentic southern hospitality experience. You won't be disappointed as there is *sum'thang* for *e'rrone* in this book. So if you're looking for some laughs while planning your trip to Texas, look no further! We've put together a list of some of the funniest things about our state. Whether you're a Texan yourself or just visiting, we promise you'll enjoy these funnies! From quirky roadside attractions to wacky festivals, these are some of the funniest places in the Lone Star State. So if you're in the mood for a little bit of fun, be sure to add these destinations to your itinerary!

Ya'll ready? Then let's get started on our journey together. It's *gonna* be one for the books...#pinkypromise.

Disclaimer: Call or check first before heading to any of these destinations, as things could have changed since the pandemic shutdown.

Chapter 1:

North Texas and the Panhandle

Adventures

Dallas Arboretum and Botanical Garden

Location: Dallas

Events and Activities: From cooking classes to flower shows and everything in between.

About:

When going to a botanical garden, *ya'll* never know what you might come across during your adventure. It's been rated as one of America's top botanical gardens to visit for a full sensory experience like no other, under cover of sunshine days and fresh air.

Quirk:

With all this being said, does someone not want to approach the President and ask him to make Arbor Day a tree-day event?

South Fork Ranch

Location: Parker

About:

So what's all the fuss about? Well, this is the place where the famous Dallas TV Show was shot all those years ago. Here you can camp, take tours and even participate in trail rides with horses as you take in the splendor of the Ewing's comings and goings.

Quirk:

Heard about the Olympian that killed Larry Hagman? He apparently shot put J.R.

Texas Motor Speedway

Location: Forth Worth

About:

If high octane, burning tires, and adrenaline are *ya'lls* thing: Then this is the place to go! There's an amazing fan suite for the ultimate behind-the-scenes experience for the whole family. Folks, it doesn't get any louder than this!

Quirk:

Have *ya'll* heard 'bout the driver that never gets a speeding ticket? It can only be a screwdriver. What else?

Tour 18

Location: Humble

About:

Folks, this place boasts all the fun *ya'll* can have on a golf course that has been designed to resemble replicas of 18 of the best golf holes in the world. Some other features to look forward to include a driving range and a putting tee.

Quirk:

With no ifs and putts, this golf course is simply tee-rific!

Woodrow House Sante Fe Caboose

Location: Lubbock

Nearby Attractions: Buddy Holly Center, Science Spectrum-Omni Tower, Cactus Theater

About:

If *ya'll* are tired of the typical *dull as Henry's bones* hotels, then there's a place just for *ya*! You've *gotta* look no further than this establishment. This family-run, quaint establishment houses its guests in a restored train caboose! It's right on track with a delicious breakfast and other luxury amenities such as a hot tub. It boasts all the comforts one can expect from southern hospitality. So come *train* or shine; they are ready to serve.

Quirk:

It's always fun sharing a one-liner train joke! Who isn't driven by the joy of monorails?

Funny Spots

Cadillac Ranch

Location: Amarillo

Type: Public art installation

About:

Along our famous Route 66 line, you'd find many roadside attractions. But one of the most notable places for a rest on *yer* journey should definitely be this spot. Here you can find anything from graffiti to wildly decorated cars and even ant farm art.

Quirk:

This place is definitely eco-blendly! LOLS!

"Eye" Sculpture

Location: Dallas

About:

Big Brother is definitely keeping an eye on *ya*! Not sure what the thinking was behind this 30-feet tall ocular marvel. Artist Tony Tasset recreated his own blue eyes in 2007 by creating a three-storey high... errr...eye! What makes this so interesting is the life-like features. It even has *'em* red veins to see.

Quirk:

Unpopular opinion: Tasset created this masterpiece because he likes to make a spectacle of himself!

Fort Worth Stockyards

Location: Fort Worth

Type: Various

Adjoining Amenities: Restaurants, bars, accommodation, events, shopping, recreational activities

About:

If *ya'll* have ever wondered what a proper cattle drive looks like, then this is the place to visit. You can expect to see cows *spread out like a cold supper with cattle drives twice daily.* The *steaks are high,* but we can promise a grand *ole* time (*cowmedian* much?) If you happen to visit on a Friday and Saturday, you'll be in a spot of luck, with their rodeo championship shows where cowboys put their hard-earned skills to the test.

Quirk:

In the 19th century, the Fort Worth Stockyards was home to the *bustlin'* livestock industry.

Palo Duro Canyon

Location: Canyon

Type: State Park

Nearby Attractions: Alibates Flint Quarries National Monument, Buffalo Lake National Wildlife Refuge, Panhandle-Plains Historical Museum

About:

Ya'll need not travel outside of the Lone State state to see some big mountains! You can visit this site, dubbed The Grand Canyon of Texas. Bring your mountain bike, horse, or walking shoe and explore the confines of this mammoth place. You can also look forward to enjoying the TEXAS Outdoor Musical, with *hill-areas* performers, which guarantees fun for the whole family!

Quirk:

This is the second-largest and second-longest of the canyons in the US. It's 20 miles wide at the widest point, 120 miles long, and sits at 3,463 feet above sea level before it drops 800 feet down.

U–Drop Inn

Location: Shamrock

Type: Cafe

Nearby Attractions: Devils Rope Museum, The Leaning Tower of Texas, 'Cast Away' Crossroads (from the movie with Tom Hanks).

About:

If *ya'll* ever find yourselves traveling along Route 66, then this establishment needs to be one of your pit stops and leg stretchers. It was built in 1936 and, like many other businesses in the area, fell into disrepair. Luckily the owners obtained a grant and restored it to its once glory days! Inside, you can expect friendly waitrons and an old-school soda fountain. Even drivers of electric cars are encouraged to visit as there is a Tesla charging station located on the premises.

Quirk:

It seems the King of rock and roll never left this building. The staff will eagerly point out to you which booth he frequented. Try it for yourself and enjoy a Martini: All shook up!

Rainbow Vomit

Location: Dallas

About:

Aesthetes unite! Art lovers near and far visit this colorful and popular site. This is a unique event for a one-of-a-kind party that'll be remembered for years to come. Their exhibits encourage audience participation by taking visitors on a journey of immersive art with many fantastic photo-taking opportunities in one place.

Quirk:

If *ya'll* be hoping to see a double rainbow, don't gold *yer* breath!

Places for the Family

Castaway Cove

Location: Wichita Falls

Attraction Type: Waterpark

About:

When the summer heat in Texas is *as hot as a $2 pistol*, you'd *wanna* make a turn here! This is the perfect establishment for kiddies' birthday parties, while mom and dad relax in one of the *cabanas* (get it?), next to the Tropical Bar with an adult beverage.

With over seven water attractions, the little cowboys and *cowgals* will be kept busy for ages digging for a proverbial *booty* we know *ain't* there. It also makes for hours of people-watching fun! We promise it's better than Walmart!

Dinosaur Valley State Park

Location: Glen Rose

About:

If you *wanna* walk the dinosaur, literally, then this is one of the places to take the young explorers for a bit of edutainment. This site was once the location where dinos have roamed the grounds. Fascinatingly enough, there are many clear, fossilized tracks on display. Of course, *nuttin'* in Texas goes down without a bit of controversy. See, the thing is, that it was first thought that some of the tracks were human. But after many back and forths, they turned out to be dinosaur footprints. Now, on the flip side of the coin, the folks down *yonder* in Glen Rose claim that some of the tracks were man-made. Either way, still a fun experience all in all and worthy of its spot on the list.

Fort Worth Zoo

Location: Fort Worth

About:

First established in 1909, those in the know have ranked the Fort Worth Zoo as the US's fifth-best zoo. Even though they only have 42 animal species, it just goes to show that dynamite can come in small packages.

Quirk:

Funny thing is: There's a rumor that this zoo even has a dog on display! Shih-Tzu not!

Thank–Giving Square

Location: Dallas

About:

Slap-bang in the middle of downtown Texas you can find a curious *lookin'* object that looks a little bit like a deconstructed, upright *croissant*. But, it's inside this pastry-*lookin'* structure where you want to go. Here, 15-feet below ground, you are transported to a beautiful urban garden that pays homage to Thanksgiving. Stained glass art, a bell tower, and the ring of thanks will renew your appreciation of being present on this earth.

Quirk:

Come to think of it? Why is stained glass so popular? Must be *'cause* it's always *lookin'* sharp…or is it shard?

Wildcatter Ranch and Resort

Location: Graham

Nearby Attractions: Possum Kingdom Lake

About:

Located a mere 90-minutes away from DFW airport, we are *as serious as the business end of a .45* when we bring you an as versatile guest ranch as it's scenic. This resort is a stone's throw away from the rugged Possum Kingdom Lake reservoir. Here you can enjoy the clearest water known to mankind. This is a dream destination of any Texan- wannabe. *Ev'thang* from guided cowboy activities, country accommodation, and hand-cut mesquite steaks can be found here — All in one beautiful place.

Quirk:

Many a rich historic event have taken place nearby this ranch, and each room is themed, depicting the tales of these occurrences. Any staff member will be more than willing to share the story around a s'more and campfire, and there is a library on-site that will transport you to a time gone by, where your inner historic will be well-satisfied.

P.S What illness can cowboys catch from their horses? Bronc-itis!

Places You Have to See

Caddo Lake

Location: Karnack

About:

With its collection of swamps and ponds, *ya'll* won't be short of adventure-seeking thrills. Stay at one of the historic ADA-friendly cabins, or take a long leisurely paddle underneath the shade of bald Cypress trees as you glide across the silky water.

Quirk:

Heard about the frog whose car broke down in the swamp? It had to be toad away!

JFK Assassination Tour

Location: Dallas

About:

There's a site in Dallas dedicated to one of our country's most-saddest moments in history. This is none other than JFK's assassination. Not only can you take a guided tour of the Oswald Rooming House, where you can see Oswald's sniper nest, but you can also view a fascinating collection of artifacts on the Sixth Floor Museum.

Quirk:

Even more than 50 years later, the conspiracy theories around the President's assassination are rife. Some include Oswald being on the CIA's payroll and even Woody Harrelson Snr. being involved. It was announced that the actor's father was a contract killer who was simultaneously executing orders on a businessman and not the President.

Six Flags

Location: Fort Worth

About:

This is a thrilling experience like no other. This is the most extensive collection of movie character-themed roller coasters in Texas. Some rides include the Batwing, the Catwoman, and even some dedicated to the carrot-eating Bugs Bunny.

Quirk:

It must be nearly impossible to enter into a relationship with a rollercoaster. There are way too many ups and downs!

The Second Amendment Cowboy

Location: Amarillo

Nearby Attractions: Floating Mesa, Cadillac Ranch, Ozymandias on the Plains

About:

What do you call a country that drives pink Cadillacs? A Pink-carnation!!

Yes, *sirree*, step right up for an attraction like no other! This is the perfect place to take some *gelfies* (gun selfies) with the likes of Elvis, Willie Nelson, and John Wayne! This is one of the best-kept secrets in Texas when it comes to roadside attractions!

Dubbed, The Muffler Man, this guy, who is also the Rifle Association's spokesperson, has created the perfect blend between vintage and paying tribute to his favorite idols from times gone by. Oh, and don't forget his prized three Cadillacs on show too!

Quirk:

P.S. The Muffler Man is a mannequin: Get it? And he has been tasked with guarding the Cadillacs. And he has been a victim in the past of numerous bullet holes! *Taco* about a tough job!

Wild Berry Farm Sunflowers

Location: Sadler

Attraction Type: Flower Farm

About:

Nuttin' brightens up a home like a vase of bright flowers. Browse their range of exotic and local fruit trees and take some home to cultivate in your own backyard.

Quirk:

After many years of trowel and error, Wild Berry Farm Sunflowers have some of the best blooms in Texas!

Chapter 2:

East Texas

———

"If you've ever driven across Texas, you know how different one area of the state can be from another. Take El Paso. It looks as much like Dallas as I look like Jack Niklaus"

- Lee Trevino (Storm, 2020).

Adventures

Air Castles by Highpoint Treehouses

Location: Ladonia

About:

The most unique place to stay in Texas! The host, Steve, has built a unique treehouse crafted from four shipping containers that boast the best in southern hospitality. Whether this is for a much-needed family break away (ages 12 and up) or for a trip in a secluded spot with your beloved, this is a must-visit destination on the list.

Quirk:

Did you hear about the house the bank gave the new branch manager? He is living in a treehouse!

Gladewater Rodeo

Location: Gladewater

About:

There's no *denyin'* that Texas is infamous for its rodeos. There is an annual event that takes place in June and is the perfect way for little wannabe cowboys and cowgals to see the riders and animals in action. Kids six years and younger will be delighted by the range of activities on offer at the Mutton Bustin event.

Quirk:

Spur on the laughter and come and join the fun. Who knows, you might even see a few ghosts in boo-ts.

Lone Star Glamp Inn

Location: Round Top

Events on Offer: Antique shows and wine festivals

About:

As we travel to the East of our state, we stumble across *lodgin's* that can only be described as glamping. Far out of reach of anything wild and boasting the most comfortable of ablutions, we present the Lone Star Glamp Inn — a unique indoor camping venue for the perfect, quick getaway.

Quirk:

Before *ya* go… what is the definition of glamping? Where you pay a fortune to live like a homeless person.

Funny Spots

Cherokee Chace Drive–Thru Safari

Location: Jacksonville

About:

Not only is this region known as the tomato capital of the world, but it also has a 300-hectare reserve, where you can view all sorts of wild animals such as Indian antelope, zebras and African longhorn cows. You can drive through the park in your own vehicle, feed some of the wildlife and then enjoy the world's largest bowl of salsa if you happen to visit the establishment in June when the tomato fest is *happenin'*.

Quirk:

What did daddy tomato say to mommy tomato? I love you from my head tomatoes!

Texas Country Music Hall of Fame

Location: Carthage

About:

This venue was established in 1998 and celebrates Texas' music stars and their contribution to country music. It's also plays host to the annual Classic Country Musical Festival. In addition, the Tex Ritter Museum is located inside the premises and was opened in 2002. Since then, it's estimated that more than 30,000 fans have visited the site to relive magical country music moments.

Quirk:

So when *ya'll* moving furniture past someone, which country singer's name do you mention? Dolly Pardon.

The Big Thicket

Location: Kountze

About:

This has to be one of Texas' most extensive ecosystem in the State. You can look forward to activities such as:

- hiking
- hunting, and
- paddling

Quirk:

Have *ya'll* ever wondered what hunters eat on a *huntin'* trip? Sour-doe bread!

Great for the Family

Beaumont

Location: East Texas

About:

History buffs unite! If *ya'll* lookin' to educate the little ones about Texan history, look no further than Beaumont. There are an array of historical sites to see here, including The Fire Museum of Texas, Saint Anthony Cathedral, and the Texas Energy Museum.

Quirk:

How do medieval beings clean their mouths? They gargoyle!

New York Texas Ziplining Adventures

Location: Larue

About:

Put the adventure back in your life and enjoy a thrilling zipline ride right here in East Texas. There are a variety of packages available to suit any budget, and you can end the day with a picnic under the shade of trees and sunshine.

Quirk:

Did you know that Yogi Bear has a love of fast cars? He was seen here recently in his Furrari!

Texas Eiffel Tower

Location: Paris

About:

Lick that calf again? Yip! *Ya'll* read that again! Just as South Africa has a town called "Parys" (Afrikaans for Paris), we here in the Lone Star state have done the same. Now, what makes ours different is that we've also erected a tower and slapped a Stetson on it, where South Africa has a dome-shaped structure in theirs!

Quirk:

We have to say that with the addition of a bright red cowboy hat, ours is *lookin' as fine as frog fur*!

Places You Have to See

Love's Lookout

Location: Jacksonville

About:

If *ya'll lookin'* for one of the most scenic rest stops in East Texas, then this place needs to be on your travel list. The structure stands at 700 feet high with benches where you can take in the magnificent scenery.

Quirk:

If a man brings a woman here, there must be a chameleon reasons he loves her!

Nacogdoches

Location: East Texas

About:

This is another piece of much-loved Texas country. It's the oldest town in our state, and it has many splendors for you to marvel at. Some of these historical sites include Millard's Crossing Historic Village, Stone Fort Museum, and Ruby M. Mize Azalea Garden, which have all been rated as top tourist attractions. So why not make a day of it and visit Caddo Indian Mounds and Lake Sam Rayburn too, for the ultimate day of outdoor fun!

Quirk:

There are so many amazing things to see in Nacogdoches; it's ranunculus!

Texas State Railroad

Location: Piney Woods

About:

This has to be one of the most scenic train rides *ya'll* could ever imagine. The steam train runs between Palestine and Rusk, and things are done exactly the same as they did in 1896. The best time to visit is during Spring, when all the flowers along the route are in full bloom.

Quirk:

Did *ya'll* ever stop to think whether trains have teeth? Of course they do; how else would they choo choo?

Taylor Rose Garden

Location: Tyler

About:

The city of Tyler has been dubbed as the nation's rose capital. And it's easy to see why. This property boasts no less than 38,000 different rose bushes and more than 500 rose varietals to admire. So it should come as no surprise that this is a popular wedding venue for many star-crossed lovers.

Quirk:

Did *ya'll* hear about the gal that was afraid of roses? To be confirmed, but apparently, she's not entirely sure where her issues stemmed from.

The World's Richest Acre

Location: Kilgore

About:

Now, this interesting-sounding name was given to the town of Kilgore due to its significant contribution to the oil sector. Even though the oil derricks have been dismantled since the '60s, it's still a pretty spectacular sight to see.

Quirk:

Did you hear about the girl who broke up with the cowboy? She found his jokes too crude.

Chapter 3:

Central and South Texas

"There's a special mystique to Texas. Texans represent many things to the uninitiated. We are bigger than life in our boots and Stetsons, rugged individualists whose two steppin' has achieved worldwide acclaim, and we were the first to define hospitality"
- Ann Richards (Storm, 2020).

Adventures

Castle Falkenstein

Location: Burnet

About:

Come and experience a *lil* bit of Bavaria, Texas-style. From fairy tale weddings to a lavish getaway, you can have it all! This entire castle can be booked with its beautiful 14,000 sq ft garden to enjoy and make your own.

Quirk:

Feel like havin' a reign-y day? Joust do it!

Commodore Perry Estate

Location: Austin

About:

Straight out of the Auberge Resorts Collection comes a historical landmark. Come and experience all the thrills and adventures of living on an Italian Renaissance Revival-style building for a historic and picturesque experience like no other!

Quirk:

By the way, have you heard about the jouster that helped out part-time at the Renaissance Fair? He was just a freelancer.

Conestoga "Glamping Wagons"

Location: Fredericksburg

About:

So, in colonial times, wagons did boast AC or heating (what a drag). Well, the good news is that you can now have the best of both worlds when you visit this establishment. This is family glamping fun to the highest degree. Kids can play on the volleyball courts, and the whole family can relax in the hot tubs after dinner.

Congress Bridge Bats

Location: Austin

About:

Have *ya'll* ever wondered what 1,500,000 bats look like, all condensed into one place? Then you have to visit the Congress Bridge Bats. This venue is home to the largest colony of urban bats in North America. This has to be one of Texas's coolest and most unusual places to visit. *Whaddya* waitin' for?

Quirk:

Have you ever wondered how batlings greet their moms? With a sound wave!

Cypress Valley

Location: Spicewood

About:

Get retrospectively transported away to your childhood by visiting this whimsical escape. Imagine a night so peaceful that *ya'll* wake up fresh and ready to take on the new day after sleeping nestled high in a treehouse amongst Cypress trees.

Quirk:

This place is so magical that you wood not believe it!

Houston Museum of Natural Science

Location: Houston

Available Exhibits: Planetarium, Observatory, and rotating exhibitions such as Body Worlds (where real cadavers are used and displayed for educational purposes).

About:

This colossal site is one of the best places to visit, with hundreds of exhibits and spaces to explore and satisfy the curious mind. You can look forward to displays like gems and minerals and even a very colorful Faberge egg exhibit.

Quirk:

If *ya'll* don't have a good time here, the yolk's on you!

Jacob's Well

Location: Wimberly

About:

Are you *feelin'* brave? Then perhaps *ya'd* like to take a trip to one of Texas' most magical swimming spots but most deadly diving locations. Rock jumping enthusiasts will revel in the thrill of jumping down into the abyss of a 30 feet deep vertical hole of nothingness.

Quirk:

What happened to the one rock jumper when he landed head first in Jacob's Well? He face-planted!

Live Oak Treehouse at HoneyTree Farm

Location: Fredericksburg

About:

It doesn't get any more romantic than this. Live Oak Treehouse as to be one of Texas's best-kept secrets when it comes to a secluded hideaway. This charming treehouse is the dream of those wanting to revel in some quiet alone time with their significant other. Talk about going out on a limb to build *somethin'* unique.

Nottingham Castle at Sherwood Forest

Location: McDade

About:

Channel your inner Robin Hood at this fascinating castle. Bet *ya'll* never thought *ya'd* get a chance to experience royal in Texas nonetheless! The castle has five bedrooms for you to book out with a group of friends. It doesn't get better than that.

Quirk:

It's speculated that after Robin and Maid Marion got married, she opened a flower shop. What did she call it? Sherwood Florist.

Funny Places

Buffalo Bayou Park Cistern

Location: Houston

About:

If you like to marvel at industrial architecture, then this 90-year old reservoir (underground) is a place you have to see at least once in your lifetime! The added bonus is when one is rushed for time but seeking a quick escape, this is the answer!

Quirk:

In essence, this considerable tank once housed 15,000,000 gallons of drinking water for Houston's inhabitants. It's so *big that it can hunt bears with a branch*!

Cathedral of Junk

Location: Austin

About:

It seems there's truth to the *sayin'* "one man's junk is another man's treasure." Austin is home to one of the most unique tourist attractions. This venue is literally made up of about 60 tons of things people didn't want anymore. Seems like a hoarder's paradise.

Quirk:

Someone is *readin'* this book right now thinking, "*I need to clear my junk drawer and donate my old batteries to this place*" Guess what? They'll even take it free of charge.

David Adickes Studio

Location: Houston

About:

Ev'thang is big in Texas, right? Yip! And randomly placed gigantic heads is no strange occurrence either. These sculptures are the work of artist David Adickes. His studio is open to the public, where one can view him and his six employees hard at work, creating the next masterpiece. His previous works include huge busts of all 43 US Presidents and even the British Invasion giants, the Beatles.

Quirk:

Do you think that David has gotten ahead of himself by any chance?

Hamilton Pool Dripping Springs

Location: Dripping Springs

About:

A beautiful natural oasis located not far from Austin. Think lining upon lining of trees encapsulating a natural spring that is just ripe for the *pickin*. Last bud not least, this is the best place in Texas to show off sunkissed skin that has received lavish helpings of cool, crisp water amid a rich ecosystem.

Marriage Island

Location: San Antonio

About:

No matter the state of *ya'll's* marriage affairs, this heart-shaped islet located in San Antonio is bound to bring some romance in the air. So why not renew your *weddin'* vows with the *ole* ball *'n* chain or enjoy reveling in newlywed couples *takin'* the plunge.

Quirk:

While penning this book, a librarian was asked if his book on wedding puns could be borrowed. Well, he immediately said "yes."

Museum of the Weird

Location: Austin

About:

Now, this place is an a-salt on the senses! Everything weird *'n* wonderful can be found here. This establishment pays tribute to the original Dime Museum that burned to the ground in 1865. One can say the phoenix always rises from the ashes when something unique is established in its place. There's *nuttin'* much else to say without spoiling the surprise. Guess you'd have to go look for *yer'self* instead.

Quirk:

Random as it sounds; one can't help but wonder how long it takes to brew a tea that tastes weird…Got it! Oolong time!

The Devil's Sinkhole

Location: Rocksprings

About:

This 400 feet deep cavern was once home to the dead from a bygone era. Native Americans believe that places like this cavern serve as a portal for the deceased to depart this earth and move on to the next. If you like the idea of bats and graffiti-laden walls penned and drawn by cowboys, then this is a must-see for an otherworldly experience.

Quirk:

Ensure that you plan properly for this visit before *ya'll's* plans fall through.

The Wilde Collection

Location: Houston

About:

If *ya'll* into the weird and wonderful, this shop of obscure things, inspired by Edgar Alan Poe and Oscar Wilde, is the place for you! At first glance upon entering the store, it appears that you've stepped into one of Terry Pratchet's books. You can expect anything from weird medical devices to freaky *lookin'* dolls that would put Chucky *'n* Annabelle to shame!

Quirk:

Think *'bout* this for a second…*Dontcha* just hate Russian dolls? They're so full of themselves!

Tower of the Americas

Location: San Antonio

About:

South Texas boasts many an architectural marvel, and the Tower of the Americas is unbeatable in many a way. Towering at 750 feet, you can get a glimpse of the splendor it offers. Visit the 4D theater and end your visit with a bite to eat at the revolving restaurant.

Quirk:

Did you ever hear about the girl who tried to climb the Tower of the Americas? Her tombstone later read, "I tried, but Eiffel off"!

Waco Mammoth Site

Location: Waco

About:

'*Twas* here that in 1978 that two gents were on the hunt for arrowheads when they made the discovery of a lifetime. You see, they stumbled upon a large bone, which they had examined by Baylor University. Later, archeological scholars would return to the site to dig, and excavated more than 24 Columbian mammoths that roamed Texas during the Ice Age.

Quirk:

As it turns out, this was a mammoth discovery! Get it? Not only is it the largest single site where prehistoric animals died from one event, but it's the only recorded site of a mammoth nursery herd.

World's Largest Killer Bee

Location: Hidalgo

About:

You simply won't *bee-lieve* your eyes when you view this gigantic Texas statue. It was in October 1990 that the first colony of killer African bees was discovered and set the United States and the rest of the world *abuzz*!

Great for the Family

1940 Air Terminal Museum

Location: Houston

About:

Once a commercial airport terminal, this venue is slowly but surely becoming a time machine to a bygone era. It was in circulation circa 1940 until 1954, when it was almost demolished but saved in 1978 by aeronautical history buffs. Since then, through hours of loving restoration and carefully adding artifacts and pieces, it's become a must-see *Texian-*landmark for all.

Quirk:

It's said that it's hard to win an argument with a pilot. But, apparently, they are known for flying out loud!

Collective Retreats

Location: Wimberley

About:

If you're lookin' for a venue for some team building activities and a break away from the office, you can take your team for a nature-boost experience here, under the Texan sky. Stay overnight in one of their tents strategically placed under juniper and oak trees but decked out in lavish luxury.

Quirk:

This is the best place to go if the rivalry at the office is getting too in-tents.

Johnson City Exotic Resort Zoo

Location: Johnson City

About:

What is a lion's favorite dance? Lion dancing!

This is *'bout* as *close enough as government work, ya'll!* Come to Africa without *leavin'* the Lone Star state. Choose between the petting zoo, a drive-through safari, or even a guided tour as one of the activities before *settlin'* in for the night by staying in one of their cabins and *bein'* woken up by lions roaring before dusk arrives.

Kettle House Galveston

Location: Galveston

About:

Takin' a trip back to the roaring '60s is what comes to mind when first *feastin' yer* eyes on this converted storage tank. Not only is it a short walk away from the beach, but it's also luxurious in every aspect with the furnishings, a vast deck, and even AC.

Quirk:

Maybe the people who used it as a storage tank are still around. Having seen its upgrade, they may have had a sense of Deja brew!

Morgan's Wonderland

Location: San Antonio

About:

This is the first theme park in the world to completely cater to differently-abled individuals and children alike. Take a ride with that special person on the carousel, ride the Wonderland Express, or let your kiddo have a swing on one of their uniquely designed swingsets. They promise a whale of a time!

SeaWorld San Antonio

Location: San Antonio

About:

Come and get your boost of Vitamin-sea when you visit this venue. Delight in the antics of the Bottlenose Dolphins, or take an exhilarating tour as you spend the day in the theme park. With so much to do, there's something to keep the whole fam busy for ages.

Stonehenge II

Location: Ingram

About:

Randomly located in a country field in Texas, it is a replica of the UK's famous Stonehenge. Come and see for *yerself* what the real Stonehenge might've looked like all those years ago, with the addition of two Easter Island moai statues.

Quirk:

Heard about the DJ that left Stonehenge? Apparently, he no longer mixes in those circles.

The Alamo

Location: San Antonio

About:

A legendary fort so infamous, it got its own movie. Many folk flock to Texas in search of a glimpse of this historic building and the story behind it. Take a guided tour, or view the exhibits dedicated to one of our country's most intense war events ever.

Quirk:

What do you call a Texan with memory loss? An ALAMO-st forgot

The Moody Gardens and Aquarium

Location: Galveston

About:

This is an all-in-one package for the whole *fam'*. Dad can enjoy a round of golf, mom can go to the spa, and the kids can explore the Aquarium and enjoy the rope and zipline courses. This is 242 acres of jam-packed fun for all.

Quirk:

Apparently, the sea life in the aquarium can sing really well. This is after they *tuna-ed* fish.

Places You Have to See

Bullock Texas State History Museum

Location: Austin

About:

If *ya'll* sitting with visitors from *outta* town and don't know what to do with them, then here's *yer* answer. What better way to entertain them than a history lesson about the origins of the Lone Star state? There's *sumthin'* for *er'body* here with a choice between the IMAX screen and many audio-visual displays for those folk that don't like *readin'*.

Quirk:

Did you know that typing while driving in Texas is not illegal? We call it Text-us. (P.S - it's just a joke, don't try it at home, or here for that matter)

Geronimo Creek Retreat

Location: New Braunfels

About:

If *ya'll* are hosting a cowboys and Indians party, then this is one of the venues to consider hosting it at. With *ev'thang* from teepees and cabins, right through to swimming, kayaking, and paddle boarding — there's no time for even one boring minute here.

Quirk:

What do you call a *cowgal livin'* in a cabin? A cabinette!

Guenther House

Location: San Antonio

About:

Now with all of these *amazin'* places to see and visit in South Texas, it's only natural that one might be *starvin'* along the way. One of the best-recommended restaurants to visit for a quick bite to eat has to be Guenther House. Enjoy a pastry and a custom roasted coffee as you take in the scenery before you. They're even nice enough to share a recipe or two!

Quirk:

If *ya'll* don't like coffee: Don't come here. You'll be labeled as a pro-caffinator!

Menger Bar

Location: San Antonio

About:

Talk a walk on the authentic Texian side when visiting The Menger Hotel's popular bar. Not only can you expect a true South Texas experience, but old-school service too. This bar is a replica of London's House of Lords Pub, and you can look forward to all the same furnishings transporting you straight to the UK without leaving America on a lengthy flight.

Quirk:

Did you hear the story of the two quotation marks who wanted a drink? They decided to walk into a "bar."

Mueller SunFlowers

Location: Austin

About:

Let it *ne'er* be said that Texas isn't technologically advanced when *lookin'* at this space. Here you can view futuristic-looking sunflowers that grow from the edge of a shopping mall. These flowers are artificial (made by man) and were designed to catch the sun's UV rays.

Quirk:

Fair *enuff'* they don't look like real flowers, but there surely is more *pressin'* matters to ponder *'bout*.

Skyspace: The Color Inside

Location: Austin

About:

This is another remarkable Texas landmark that can't be missed. The best times to visit are either sunrise or sunset. Here you can view Turell's light sequences, with each set lasting about 60 minutes in total.

Quirk:

Have you heard about the skunk that fell from the sky? Everybody ran because they thought it was a stink bomb!

S.S. Selma

Location: Galveston

About:

During the WWII steel shortage, it was ordered that ships had to be built from concrete. One such vessel is still on display a mile off the Galveston coast. Reachable only by boat, this decaying structure has a rich history. It was only one of 12 commissioned ships that were ever completed and ready to deploy to battle. Sadly, Selma only served for a year after being hit and sent to an early grave. Years later, she got a second chance when federal agents used her steamer to destroy illegal contraband from bootleggers. What does this mean? Well, let's just say that more than 11,000 bottles of liquor got smashed against the concrete ship.

Quirk:

Can the bootlegger's ghosts still be around consuming spirits? Hmmmm…they probably then get sheet-faced!

The Bloomhouse

Location: West Austin

About:

Well, this one's *kinda* hard to explain. But in short, it's a unicorn seashell house. Must come as no surprise that this was the brainchild of two hippy students from the '70s (if *y'all cathin'* the drift). This house will seriously challenge yer logic since there is no straight line inside this architectural marvel. Best of all, you can even stay here for a night or two. One can't help to wonder if you can then still hear the ocean inside this shell?

Quirk:

So all jokes set aside…did you know that Scotland's national animal is the unicorn? Just some useless pub quiz trivia to share.

Twilight Epiphany Skyspace

Location: Houston

About:

Created by artist James Turrel, this is another bucket list stop requiring more than one visit. This perfectly designed kinetic space marvel changes color and feel with each of Earth's daily rotations. No day is the same when it comes to the effect taking place right before *yer* eyes.

Quirk:

Did you hear about the time when burgers were falling out of the Texan sky? Climatologists called it a meatier shower.

Chapter 4:

West Texas

———

"I've traveled all over the world, but I don't think there is any place better than Texas"
- Red Adair (Storm, 2020).

Adventures

Basecamp Terlingua

Location: Terlingua

About:

You literally have four different options when it comes to *choosin'* your accommodations here. Pick between:

- bubbles
- campsites
- casitas
- lotus tents
- retro trailers
- *Tipis* (teepees)

As if that's not *enuff* the Big Bend National park is located a stone's throw away, providing you with the adventure of a lifetime.

Quirk:

Have you *e'er* wondered why the sky is blue? Must be *'cause* no one is *askin'* how it's *feelin'*.

Davis Mountains State Park

Location: Fort Davis

About:

If you need a break away from the rat race of life, then this site is the place for you. With some of the most scenic views in Texas, it's easy to see why this is one of our state's most popular tourist attractions. So visit them, and don't sweat the tall stuff!

Presidio County Courthouse

Location: Marfa

About:

This historical landmark is the stuff of dreams for any architecture lover and was built in 1886 at the cost of $60,000. Assigned landmark status in 1964, this building resembles the El Paso courthouse, designed by the same mastermind.

Quirk:

Have *ya'll* heard about the designer that makes the attire lawyers wear to court? She called her collection "law suits."

The Gage Hotel

Location: Marathon

About:

Constructed in 1927, The Gage Hotel is one of the oldest landmarks in Marathon. The hotel is historical, and the rooms are amazing, but it's their bar that boasts the highest accolade of apparently serving the best margaritas in Texas (according to Saveur magazine).

Quirk:

Before *ya'll* look too deeply into *yer* Pear Tequilas, just remember not to drive im-pear-ed…it's frowned upon *'ere.*

The Hotel Paisano

Location: Marfa

About:

One of the top reasons to make a stop 'ere, is for the Memorabilia room. This hotel was once home to movie giants Elizabeth Taylor, James Dean, and Rock Hudson while filming the movie "Giant." For some, it will be as close as we can get to movie stars and tracing their footsteps.

Quirk:

Did you hear what Elizabeth Taylor had to say about six-star hotels? Well, to be honest, she feels they are completely overrated!

Funny Places

Boquillas International Ferry

Location: Big Bend National Park

About:

Take a trip to the other side (Mexico) when you spend a day outdoors and start your journey at the Boquillas International Ferry departure point. From there, you can hire a *burro*, truck, or a horse and spend the day in the sunshine before *headin'* back home. The ferry departs daily from Big Bend National Park on the southeastern border and takes visitors across the Rio Grande into Coahuila, Mexico. It takes all of one minute to get from one side to the next.

Quirk:

Did you know there is a Pokèmon with origins in Mexico? It's called the Zikachu!

Casa de Azucar

Location: El Paso

About:

Now, the first thing that strikes *ya* when you hit this site is the fact that the building looks like it's been made of Mentos. Sometimes referred to as the Sugar House, *ya'll* be tempted to take a lick…let this be at *yer* own peril!

Quirk:

By the way, it was recently discovered that Mentos go to the amuse-mint park for fun. Now *ya* know!

Caverns of Sonora

Location: Sonora

About:

If you don't have a fear of enclosed spaces (claustrophobia), then the Caverns of Sonora come highly recommended. There are many tiny rooms to explore in these caves, and after a long day of spelunking, what better way to pitch up a tent and spend the night under the stars?

Quirk:

It should come as no surprise that the tour guides wear special pants during guided tours. They're called Stalac-tights!

Marfa Mystery Lights Viewing Center

Location: Marfa

About:

Most commonly known as the Marfa ghost lights, this phenomenon can be observed on Route 67. However, the best place to get a good look is apparently on the shoulder of Highway 90, plus minus 90 miles east of Marfa.

Quirk:

It's believed that light bulbs maintain a strict diet in order to maintain their svelte figures. But, apparently, they prefer to live on light snacks.

Prada Marfa

Location: Marfa (ok, not really. It's actually in Valentine)

About:

Fashionistas will both rejoice and swear at this notion at the same time. It's a Prada store fully stocked and located in the middle of nowhere. The sad thing about this is that the shop never opens. Another interesting fact is that after the store was vandalized, the owners decided to keep the leftover stock, but with some adjustments. All the shoes are right-footed, and the bags don't have bottoms. Serves *'em* right!

Quirk:

Here's to *wonderin'* if those criminals are Prada themselves

Star Party at the Mcdonald Observatory

Location: Observatory

About:

By *makin'* use of no less than five telescopes, *ya'll* now have the unique opportunity to treat *yerself* to one of Mcdonald Observatory's famous Star Parties. Every Tuesday, Friday, and Saturday evening, you can view a number of sparkly celestial objects in focus.

Quirk:

A friend recently took his bird for a date night here. Let's just say she was *o'er* the moon with the experience.

Great for the Family

Guadalupe Mountains National Park

Location: Salt Flat

About:

Whether *yer* after a hike in nature, a spot of shopping, or seeking a scouts group/junior ranger program to join, this National Park has it all. The infamous Devil's Hall will truly test *yer* endurance with this strenuity level.

Quirk:

What did the ranger say about his work during an interview? He said it was a walk in the park.

Indian Lodge

Location: Fort Davis

About:

With a breathtaking view of the Davis Mountains and the stark contrast of the white adobe walls, it makes for a venue that truly stands out from the rest. So bring the working folk here for a breakaway session or the family for some time out away from screens. There's, of course, WiFi available in hotspots located all around the lodge, but not in the actual rooms.

Quirk:

After the mountain broke up with his girlfriend, he was left in despair for days. Apparently, he had a hard time *gettin' o'er* it.

Places You Have to See

Buggy Barn Museum

Location: Blanco

About:

Did you know you can now travel back to the 1860s to 1900s without the use of a time machine? Let's face it equine-drawn transportation was a big thing back then. This museum has many displays of carriages, buggies, and wagons, all dating back to when it used to be a daily site and not so much a novelty as they are today.

Quirk:

Apparently, the people visiting here like to wave to other visitors. That's why they call it a hey-ride!

Chinati Hot Springs

Location: Presidio

About:

Come and experience all the quiet splendor that the Chihuahuan Mountains and desert have to offer. This is probably the most remote location in this entire book. You can expect to have the most magnificent view of the stars as you relax in natural hot springs.

Quirk:

Based on all the reviews, it appears that this place is simply out-sandding!

El Paso Museum of Art

Location: El Paso

About:

Don't be fooled in *thinkin'* that for its size this establishment won't rock your socks off! The museum is located in an old Greyhound Station and boasts no less than 7,000 pieces of art and artifacts. The works span from the Byzantine era to the present, with masterpieces on display from prominent artists such as Botticelli and Canaletto. Art lovers will delight in the fact that there's no entrance fee.

Quirk:

It's said that this region has the best quarterback in the United States. What's his name? El Paso!

Fort Leaton State Historic Site

Location: Presidio

About:

Ya'll get instant feelings of what it had to be like in the 1800s when visiting this historic landmark. This once large, imposing building rests among the many archeological sites being studied and excavated. It's also centrally located for easy access to other nature and hiking trails such as Big Bend National Park and Copper Canyon.

Quirk:

Apparently, there's a woman who gave birth in this park. She called the kid "Ranch," *'cause* he be *dressin'*.

Guadalupe Peak

Location: Culberson County

About:

What is so unique about this place *ya'll?* Well, it's the highest point in our Lone Star state. It's categorized with a metal pyramid. This structure was erected in 1958 by American Airlines to mark the 100th anniversary of none other than the Butterfield Overland Mail Trail, which passed on the southern side of the mountain.

Quirk:

It's said that after climbing this site, you'll have a little less attitude and a little more altitude!

Monahans Sandhill State Park

Location: Monahans

About:

With Mother Nature *puttin'* her best foot forward, *ya'll* be spoilt for choice when visiting this site. Kids will delight in playing among the sand dunes, and the patterns produced on the sand by the wind are a sight to behold.

Quirk:

It begs the question...Does Monahans Sandhill State Park accept payment in the form of sand dollars?

Starlight Theater Restaurant and Saloon

Location: Terlingua

About:

This restaurant-come-saloon establishment is one of Terlingua's most frequented tourist destinations. It's located about 12 miles from the border of Mexico and is deemed as a bit of a "ghost town." So sit down to enjoy their cold, crisp *brewski's* and their flavorful Tex-Mex food, all to the strum of bluegrass music.

Quirk:

Be on the lookout for the hordes of bunnies that like to visit during hoppy hour!

Chapter 5:

Texas Boondocking and RV Venues

———

"You know you're a Texan when...the best parking space is determined by shade instead of distance"

(Crandall, n.d.).

Big Bend National Park

Location: West Texas

About:

Now, folks, the Chihuahuan Desert is just waiting to spoil you with her *breathtakin'* views of the Rio Grande. It's kinda hard to believe that this is an excellent spot for RV *boondockin'*. Of course, this might not be for everybody due to its remote location. But if *ya'll* dare, then you can look forward to bird *watchin'*, and *hikin'* on beautiful trails through the canyons, mountains, and desert. Before *comin'* here, ensure that you are equipped with a silent RV generator, as there is no electricity on offer. It sounds like one of the best spots for stargazing in all of Texas.

Quirk:

What do you call a bird watcher that likes to tell jokes? A comedi-hen.

Boulton Lake Campground

Location: Zavalla

About:

If *ya'll* feeling' along the adventurous line, then this is right up *yer* alley, or is it pathway? With miles of quiet and remote trails to explore, the chances are high that you might very well have the entire campground to *yerselves.*

Quirk:

This sounds like the perfect place to release some tent-sion.

Crystal Beach Campground

Location: Bolivar (well, close to it anyway)

About:

This is another opportunity that you can't miss to camp out on the beach while you play around in the Mexican Gulf. You can pick your perfect spot from 27 miles of unspoiled beachfront. The fire station behind the beach also offers free public showers, and porta-potties are scattered on the beach. There are no actual roads to drive on, but why not let the tires of the RV feel the white sand in its folds?

Quirk:

Beach, fires, and s'mores? It sounds like the perfect match!

Elephant Mountain Wilderness Management Area

Location: 60 minutes north of Big Bend

About:

This place is all about the views and activities on offer. Apart from exploring Elephant Mountain, *ya'll* can also look forward to biking, hiking, and jeep trails. There are no amenities here, but that's not always a bad *thang.* Sometimes, we need to just get away from it all for a while.

Quirk:

P.S. If you're 17 and older, *ya'll* need a usage stamp. But, hey, don't flame the messenger!

Fort Anahuac Park

Location: Galveston Bay

About:

Bird watchers and sea lovers will revel while boondocking at this site, and if *yer* a boating enthusiast; even better. There are plenty of historical markers to admire and birdlife to see. If *ya'll* are lucky, you can even watch a softball or baseball game.

Quirk:

Let's go boondocking! Alpaca my sleeping bag.

Fritch Fortress

Location: Fritch

About:

This secret hideaway is located inside the recreational park of Lake Meredith. Its ideal location and setting provide ample opportunity for a spot of fishing or boating. In addition, it has a free dump station and areas where you can fill up the water tanks. Finally, enjoy the ultimate *al fresco* dining experience at their picnic shelters and grilling stations, not to mention their clean ablution facilities.

Quirk:

Here, it seems that you can have your kayak and eat it too!

Grapevine Hills Primitive Roadside Campsites

Location: Big Bend National Park

About:

Here, each site has its own gravel parking pad. Unfortunately, there are no complimentary or otherwise services available, and *ya'll* also need a backcountry camping permit. However, all the activities on offer more than make up for it. This includes scenic driving, hiking, biking, and even kayaking. What a way to get closer to nature?

Quirk:

This place will make you one happy camper!

Huber City Park

Location: Borger

About:

This is probably one of the only Texas *boondockin'* sites where you have access to electricity while camping on one of their eight designated sites. *Ya'll* permitted to stay for up to 72 hours within seven days at a time. Even though there are no sewer or water hookups, they make up for it with the water facilities and free dump station site.

Quirk:

Can you bear the large number of excellent puns in this book?

McBride Canyon and Mullinaw Creek Camp

Location: Amarillo

About:

This site is not just a mouthful, but it's one of the most organized rigs in Texas for boondockers! The camping pads are level, the ablution facilities are superb, and the site is a short drive away from all things adventure-related for the outdoorsy.

Quirk:

It seems like this place has a sound chip on its smolder.

Open Air Resorts

Location: New Braunfels, South Texas

About:

With this pet-friendly establishment, you can now bring Fido or Fluffy along without worrying about their accommodations elsewhere. So pack your RV for an adventurous getaway like no other. Activities on offer include a fishing pond, clubhouse, and even a pickleball court.

Quirk:

Ever wondered how many people it takes to change an RV's light bulb? Unfortunately, it can only be one…the rest are busy *dealin'* with grey water problems.

Port Aransas Beach

Location: Port Aransas

About:

Before you enter, you'll need to purchase an annual permit. However, this will give you access to many sites, including this beach — all for one nominal fee. In addition, you get to park right up close to the beach for a truly unspoiled view of the waves. You can stay here for up to 72 hours, and it's promised that *ya'll* will leave refreshed and ready for the road trip ahead.

Quirk:

The only thing left to ask is wood you like to go camping?

Ray and Donna West Free RV Park

Location: Muleshoe

About:

Located in the City of Muleshoe comes the Ray and Donna West Free RV Park. This site has all the trimmings. Not only are the camping pads located in the asphalt parking area, but there is access to free water, electricity, and even a sewer hookup (plus a free RV dump station too). You can stay here for three days at a time and leave a donation for the owners to maintain it in tip-top shape.

Quirk:

Can't *ya'll* already hear the kids asking…RV there yet?

Sam Rose Collins Recreational Park

Location: Burkeville

About:

With a beautiful scenic panorama of Toledo Bend, you'd be amazed at the array of activities on offer here. Canoeing and delectable Cajun cuisine are what come to mind, with fun for the whole family. Then, nestle in for the night amongst the mammoth pine trees and animals as the wind transports you to dreamland.

Quirk:

So good, but Canjun handle it, is the question.

Scheiner City Park

Location: Junction

About:

If *ya'll* looking for peace and quiet with a view of the Llano River, then this is a must-visit stop on your Texas exploration journey. Here, you can park the RV right next to the river banks for some kayaking and even *swimmin'*. Then, why not head into town for the night for a good ole boogey at the London Hall for a glimpse of small-town America.

Quirk:

Not sure if the rumors are to be believed, but whispers were heard that ducks could be seen doing the quackstep at London Hall. Why not go see for *yerself?*

Silverton Municipal Park

Location: Panhandle Texas

About:

This is another one of a few Texas gems that have both water and electricity facilities for RV hookups. All the camping pads are level and constructed from gravel, and each one even has its own little grass yard. This park is located 60 minutes from northern Amarillo, with a population of fewer than 1,000 inhabitants.

Quirk:

With all the beauty and splendor on offer, *y'all* want to boondock forest of *yer* life!

Conclusion

———

> *"Most Americans can cover their home state in less than a week. In Texas, if you concentrate and work at it steadily, you can traverse your territory by about age thirty-seven."*
> **- Rosemary Kent (Storm, 2020).**

In Texas, we aren't just known for our impressive statistics! Perhaps it has *sumthin'* to do with ole Bobby and JR Ewing and the rest of the 'Dallas' folk, way back in the '80s. By now, *ya'll* should have tummy aches from *laughin'* and should be packin' yer bags for a long, extended trip through this magical 28th state of the US.

When traveling through Texas, you can expect to see anything from bearded hipsters, cowboy wannabees, and even beach bums with bleached hair. You'll get to see things like expansive ranch lands all the way through to balmy Gulf Coast water and splendid views. It's also known that driving in Texas is the most common way of navigating through this vast state, and with the boondocking options at your disposal, you'll be genuinely spoilt for choice.

It's highly recommended that you plan your trip carefully since trekking takes time from one place to the next. Therefore it's definitely worthwhile to stop along the many roadside attractions and consult the book preceding this one for great places to eat. After all, when traveling with the whole family, a road trip is the most convenient for all parties concerned.

With Austin as the capital of Texas, it's also worth mentioning that it's one of the safest cities to travel to in the whole of America. Not to mention the "Keep Austin Weird" bumper stickers…it just says it all (meaning *ya'll* in for a good time).

If you find yourself in Texas and want to see some of the more "interesting" tourist destinations, then be sure to check out this list. Just be warned, if you do make it out to these places, you may get a few strange looks from the locals. But, we've got you covered with our roundup of the most must-see spots in the Lone Star State. There's something for everyone on this list, from charming small towns to exciting big cities.

Please, feel free to let us know if we missed any must-see venues – we always love exploring new areas! Thanks for reading, and happy travels!

A Special Gift To Our Readers

Included in your purchase of this book, we are giving you a fun information book on Texas Slang, Sayings and the History of where they come from. We hope that you like it!

Click on the link below and let us know which email address to deliver it to:

www.funnytravellist.com

Our Website

Enjoy this book?

Honest reviews of my books are the only thing that helps bring attention of my books to other readers. I don't have the money to throw at advertising. Not yet anyway. So, If you enjoyed this book, I would be grateful if you could spend just 3 minutes leaving a review (It can be as short as you like).

The review button is on the upper left corner of our website. Just scan the code above and look upper left. - Thank you very much.

Facebook Group
WELCOME TO THE GATHERING!

If you want to get even more informative insight on Funny Travel Lists, you can always join our Facebook group. Our group includes: Travelers, Boon Dockers, Campers, RV Enthusiast, New Texans and Adventurers. This group was set up to discuss exploring funny and unique places and tell the stories of what we have come across in the US. We are a tight community seeking additional secret adventures while sharing some of our success and failures out on the road. We discuss all types of subjects and many that the general public are unaware! Stop by and see if we have a Funny Travel List book for your state! Be nice and share in the spirit of helping!

The Funny Travel List Group

www.facebook.com/groups/funnytravellist/

Scan the QR code to easily get to the group

References

360Wichita. (2016, July 11). *Keeper of the Plains history.* 360Wichita. https://www.360wichita.com/blog/Local/Keeper-of-the-Plains-History.html

Adebowale, T. (2021, June 2). 143 climbing puns and mountain puns that will not leave you Everest. Kidadl. https://kidadl.com/articles/climbing-puns-and-mountain-puns-that-will-not-leave-you-everest

Airbnb. (n.d.-a). *airbnb: Vacation rentals, cabins, beach houses, unique homes & experiences.* Airbnb. https://www.airbnb.co.za/rooms/plus/28386163?source_impression_id=p3_1645183409_XXa2%2BRzHkiOfSbT2

Airbnb. (n.d.-b). *airbnb: Vacation rentals, cabins, beach houses, unique homes & experiences.* Airbnb. https://www.airbnb.co.za/rooms/34602890?source_impression_id=p3_1641622849_vX6owyUvMJIAxUbA&locale=en&_set_bev_on_new_domain=1645252048_YTU1OGIwZjE4Nzhl

Airbnb. (n.d.-c). *airbnb: Vacation rentals, cabins, beach houses, unique homes & experiences.* Airbnb. https://www.airbnb.co.za/rooms/41124318/?locale=en&_set_bev_on_new_domain=1645252048_YTU1OGIwZjE4Nzhl&source_impression_id=p3_1645438754_zWqWJDKSURVXJ2oD

Airbnb. (n.d.-d). *airbnb: Vacation rentals, cabins, beach houses, unique homes & experiences.* Airbnb. https://www.airbnb.co.za/rooms/37247447?source_impression_id=p3_1641621089_wuhVNYD1pWfMkaa9&guests=1&adults=1&locale=en&_set_bev_on_new_domain=1645252048_YTU1OGIwZjE4Nzhl

Airbnb. (n.d.). *airbnb: vacation rentals, cabins, beach houses, unique homes & experiences.* Airbnb. https://www.airbnb.co.za/rooms/39032564?locale=en&_set_bev_on_new_domain=1645182782_YzU0YzEzYjQwYjQw&source_impression_id=p3_1645182784_%2Fl%2BxxetD38Hf1cbj

American Sky. (n.d.). *A beginner's guide to Texas.* American Sky. https://www.americansky.co.uk/texas-holidays/a-beginner-s-guide-to-texas

Atlas Obscura. (2010, April 7). *Prada Marfa*. Atlas Obscura. htt
atlasobscura.com/places/prada-marfa

Atlas Obscura. (n.d.). *Relive the magic of Route 66 travel at U-Drop Inn.* Atlas
https://www.atlasobscura.com/places/udrop-inn

Atlas Obscura. (n.d.). *Stonehenge II.* Atlas Obscura. https://www.atlas
com/places/stonehenge-ii

Atlas Obscura. (n.d.). *Texas Eiffel Tower.* Atlas Obscura. https://www.atlasobscu.
com/places/texas-eiffel-tower

Atlas Obscura. (n.d.). *Thanks-Giving Square.* Atlas Obscura. https://www.
atlasobscura.com/places/thanks-giving-square

Atlas Obscura. (n.d.). *The Devil's Sinkhole.* Atlas Obscura. https://www.atlasobscura.
com/places/the-devils-sinkhole-rocksprings-texas

Atlas Obscura. (n.d.). *The Second Amendment Cowboy.* Atlas Obscura. https://www.
atlasobscura.com/places/the-second-amendment-cowboy

Atlas Obscura. (n.d.). *The Wilde Collection.* Atlas Obscura. https://www.
atlasobscura.com/places/the-wilde-collection-houston-texas

Atlas Obscura. (n.d.). *Twilight Epiphany Skyspace.* Atlas Obscura. https://www.
atlasobscura.com/places/twilight-epiphany-skyspace

Atlas Obscura. (n.d.). *S. S. Selma.* Atlas Obscura. https://www.atlasobscura.com/
places/s-s-selma

Atlas Obscura. (n.d.). *Waco Mammoth Site.* Atlas Obscura. https://www.atlasobscura.
com/places/waco-mammoth-site

Atlas Obscura. (n.d.). *1940 Air Terminal Museum.* Atlas Obscura. https://www.
atlasobscura.com/places/1940-air-terminal-museum

Atlas Obscura. (n.d.). *A sweet labor of love.* Atlas Obscura. https://www.atlasobscura.
com/places/casa-de-azucar

Atlas Obscura. (n.d.). *Buffalo Bayou Park Cistern.* Atlas Obscura. https://www.
atlasobscura.com/places/buffalo-bayou-park-cistern

Atlas Obscura. (n.d.). *Cathedral of Junk.* Atlas Obscura. https://www.atlasobscura.
com/places/cathedral-junk

\s Obscura. (n.d.). *Dallas "Eye" Sculpture.* Atlas Obscura. https://www.atlasobscura.com/places/eye-sculpture

Atlas Obscura. (n.d.). *David Adickes Studio.* Atlas Obscura. https://www.atlasobscura.com/places/david-adickes-sculpture-gallery

Atlas Obscura. (n.d.). *Guadalupe Peak.* Atlas Obscura. https://www.atlasobscura.com/places/guadalupe-peak

Atlas Obscura. (n.d.). *Museum of the Weird.* Atlas Obscura. https://www.atlasobscura.com/places/museum-weird

Atlas Obscura. (n.d.). *Mueller SunFlowers.* Atlas Obscura. https://www.atlasobscura.com/places/mueller-sunflowers

Atlas Obscura. (n.d.). *Hamilton Pool.* Atlas Obscura. https://www.atlasobscura.com/places/hamilton-pool

Atlas Obscura. (n.d.). *Dinosaur Valley State Park.* Atlas Obscura. https://www.atlasobscura.com/places/dinosaur-valley-state-park-2

Atlas Obscura. (n.d.). *Jacob's Well.* Atlas Obscura. https://www.atlasobscura.com/places/jacob-s-well

Atlas Obscura. (n.d.). *Congress Bridge Bats.* Atlas Obscura. https://www.atlasobscura.com/places/austin-congress-bridge-bats

Basecamp Terlingua. (n.d.). *Basecamp Terlingua.* Basecamp Terlingua. https://basecampterlingua.com/

Beano. (2021, July 14). *20 weird jokes odder than a custard shoe.* Beano. https://www.beano.com/posts/weird-jokes

Beech Estate Campsite. (2015, November 4). *Our favourite jokes about camping.* Beech Estate Campsite. https://pegsandpitches.co.uk/beech-estate/news/jokes-about-camping/

Blake, S. (2021, July 20). *70 beach puns that shore are good.* Kidadl. https://kidadl.com/articles/beach-puns-that-shore-are-good

Botanica Wichita. (2019, September 23). *Botanica – Community Gardens in Wichita Kansas.* Botanica Wichita. https://botanica.org/

Buggy Barn Museum. (n.d.). *Buggy Barn Museum.* Buggy Barn Museum. http://www.buggybarnmuseum.com/

Castaway Cove Water Park. (n.d.). *Wichita Falls Water Park | Fun birthdays &*
group outings | Castaway Cove. Castaway Cove Water Park. https://www.
castawaycovewaterpark.com/

Castle Falkenstein. (n.d.). *Castle Falkenstein.* Castle Falkenstein. https://
castlefalkensteintx.com/

Caverns of Sonora. (n.d.). *Welcome to the Caverns of Sonora.* Caverns of Sonora.
http://www.cavernsofsonora.com/

Chapman, R. (2019, March 21). *40 puns about Spring that are blooming with good vibes.*
EliteDaily.   https://www.elitedaily.com/p/40-puns-about-spring-that-are-
blooming-with-good-vibes-16976693

Chinati Hot Springs. (n.d.). *Chinati Hot Springs.* Chinati Hot Springs. https://www.
chinatihotsprings.net/

Clarke, D. (2021, April 28). *66 sunflower puns that stand out.* Kidadl. https://kidadl.
com/articles/sunflower-puns-that-stand-out

Collective Retreats. (n.d.). *Austin Glamping & Resort in Texas Hill Country.* Collective
Retreats.   https://www.collectiveretreats.com/retreat/collective-hill-
country/

Commodore Perry Estate. (n.d.). *Commodore Perry Estate.* Commodore Perry Estate.
https://www.expedia.com/Austin-Hotels-Commodore-Perry-Estate-An-
Auberge-Resort.h42070171.Hotel-Information?AID=11873095&PID=917
7461&URL=https://www.expedia.com/Austin-Hotels-Commodore-Perry-
Estate-An-Auberge-Resort.h42070171.Hotel-Information&affcid=network.
cj.9177461.11873095.&cjevent=9569a48d704b11ec820c00130a180514

Crandall, D. (n.d.). *You know you're a Texan when... | Texas humor, Texans, only in Texas.*
Pinterest. https://za.pinterest.com/pin/227642956135397270/

Cypress Valley. (n.d.). *Cypress Valley - Texas Hill Country Treehouse & Ranch Retreat.*
Cypress Valley. https://www.cypressvalley.com/

Dallas Arboretum and Botanical Garden. (n.d.). *Visit the Dallas Arboretum and*
Botanical Garden. Dallas Arboretum and Botanical Garden. https://www.
dallasarboretum.org/visitor-information/

Dave. (2020, June 9). *101+ quotes about Texas | Fun, famous & short Texas quotes.* Jones
around the World. https://www.jonesaroundtheworld.com/quotes-about-
texas/

Dingus, A. (1994, December 1). *More colorful Texas sayings than you can shake a stick at.* TexasMonthly. https://www.texasmonthly.com/being-texan/more-colorful-texas-sayings-than-you-can-shake-a-stick-at/

Down to Scuba. (2021, February 1). *The best scuba diving jokes.* Down to Scuba. https://www.downtoscuba.com/the-best-scuba-diving-jokes/

El Paso Museum of Art. (n.d.). *El Paso Museum of Art.* El Paso Museum of Art. https://epma.art/

Exploration Place. (n.d.). *Exhibits.* Exploration Place. https://exploration.org/exhibits/

FortWorth Stockyards. (n.d.). *Fort Worth Stockyards.* FortWorth Stockyards. https://www.fortworthstockyards.org/

Frost, M. (2021a, April 27). *40 dance puns that you'll want to twist and shout about.* Kidadl. https://kidadl.com/articles/dance-puns-that-youll-want-to-twist-and-shout-about

Frost, M. (2021b, May 4). *41 train puns that are right on track.* Kidadl. https://kidadl.com/articles/train-puns-that-are-right-on-track

Geronimo Creek Retreat. (n.d.). *Geronimo Creek Retreat.* Geronimo Creek Retreat. https://geronimocreekretreat.com/

Giroux, M. (2021, May 28). *50 funny mountain puns.* A Broken Backpack. https://abrokenbackpack.com/puns-about-mountains/

Green, A. (2020, July 23). *33 actually funny camping puns that will reduce tent-sion.* Eternal Arrival. https://eternalarrival.com/camping-puns/

Guadalupe Mountains National Park. (2017). *Guadalupe Mountains National Park (U.S. National Park Service).* Guadalupe Mountains National Park. https://www.nps.gov/gumo/index.htm

Guenther House. (n.d.). *Guenther House.* Guenther House. https://www.guentherhouse.com/

Houston Museum of Natural Science. (n.d.). *Visit.* Houston Museum of Natural Science. https://www.hmns.org/visit/

Howdy-RV. (2019, June 17). *5 great RV boondocking spots in Texas.* Howdy-RV. https://www.howdyrv.com/blog/5-great-rv-boondocking-spots-in-texas--14364

Inn, L. S. G. (n.d.). *Welcome to the Great Indoors...* Lone Star Glamp Inn. https://lonestarglampinn.com/

Jokes4US. (n.d.). *Alcohol jokes - Alcoholic jokes.* Jokes4US. http://www.jokes4us.com/dirtyjokes/alcoholjokes.html

Jokes4Us. (n.d.). *Texas jokes - State jokes.* Jokes4Us. http://www.jokes4us.com/miscellaneousjokes/worldjokes/texasjokes.html

Keep Laughing Forever. (2022). *The best zoo puns for 2022.* Keep Laughing Forever. https://www.keeplaughingforever.com/zoo-puns

Kidadl. (n.d.). *40+ best desert puns that are out-sand-ing.* Kidadl. https://kidadl.com/articles/best-desert-puns-that-are-out-sand-ing

Kidadl. (n.d.). *41 best train jokes for kids.* Kidadl. https://kidadl.com/articles/best-train-jokes-for-kids

Kidadl. (2020, December 20). *51+ best mountain puns that will have you yodeling.* Kidadl. https://kidadl.com/articles/best-mountain-puns-that-will-have-you-yodeling

Kidadl. (2021, May 14). *90+ best zoo puns that go wild.* Kidadl. https://kidadl.com/articles/best-zoo-puns-that-go-wild

Kidadl. (2021, August 3). *60 best sand puns that make waves.* Kidadl. https://kidadl.com/articles/best-sand-puns-that-make-waves

Kidadl. (2021, August 5). *85+ light puns that will light up any room.* Kidadl. https://kidadl.com/articles/light-puns-that-will-light-up-any-room

Kidadl. (2021, August 23). *35 best flying puns that are sky-high.* Kidadl. https://kidadl.com/articles/best-flying-puns-that-are-sky-high

Kingsley, J. (2021, November 4). *33 cowboy puns that will make you go horse with laughter.* Kidadl. https://kidadl.com/articles/cowboy-puns-that-will-make-you-go-horse-with-laughter

LaffGaff. (2020, August 17). *25 hilarious butterfly jokes and puns!* LaffGaff. https://laffgaff.com/butterfly-jokes-puns/

Lodgewell. (n.d.). *The Bloomhouse by Lodgewell | West Austin vacation rental.* Lodgewell. https://www.lodgewell.co/thebloomhouse

McDonald Observatory. (n.d.). *Evening Program: Star parties.* McDonald Observatory. https://mcdonaldobservatory.org/visitors/programs/evening-programs

Moody Gardens. (n.d.). *Hotel & amusement theme parks | Houston attractions | Family & group vacation ideas TX.* Moody Gardens. https://www.moodygardens.com/

Morgan's Wonderland. (n.d.). *The world's first ultra-accessible[TM] theme park.* https://morganswonderland.com/

Mortons on the Move. (2022, January 10). *10 best places for boondocking in Texas.* Mortons on the Move. https://www.mortonsonthemove.com/boondocking-in-texas/

Munden, E. (2021, May 14). *65 wedding puns that will have you crying with laughter.* Kidadl. https://kidadl.com/articles/wedding-puns-that-will-have-you-crying-with-laughter

Museum of World Treasures. (n.d.). *Museum of World Treasures.* Museum of World Treasures. https://worldtreasures.org/?gclid= CjwKCAiAgbiQBhAHEiwAuQ6Bkuf70pECRKWZbgAqXm66fOH10Vn6pGbSSX1QZxWxKWc6gQZLewcUyxoCQUAQAvD_BwE

Newman, D. (2022, January 24). *70 funny mountain puns & mountain jokes to make you laugh.* What's Danny Doing? https://www.whatsdannydoing.com/blog/mountain-puns-mountain-jokes

Newport Grill. (n.d.). *Newport Grill.* Newport Grill. https://www.newportgrill.com/location/newport-grill/

Open Air Resorts. (n.d.). *Open Air Resorts Luxury RV Resort, Glamping & RV Park Texas.* Open Air Resorts. https://www.openairrv.com/

Pennington, D. (2019, June 26). *The absolute best RV jokes. Period.* Outdoorsy. https://www.outdoorsy.com/blog/best-rv-jokes

Punpedia. (n.d.). *Faberge.* Punpedia. https://punpedia.org/tag/faberge/

Puns and One Liners. (2020, January 10). *Kettle jokes.* Puns and One Liners. https://punsandoneliners.com/randomness/kettle-jokes/

Punstoppable. (n.d.-a). *26 hilarious wagon puns.* Punstoppable. https://punstoppable.com/Wagon-puns

Punstoppable. (n.d.-b). *26 hilarious wagon puns.* Punstoppable. https://punstoppable.

com/Wagon-puns

Punstoppable. (n.d.). *3 hilarious El Paso puns.* Punstoppable. https://punstoppable. com/el-paso-puns

Punstoppable. (n.d.). *6 hilarious Stonehenge puns.* Punstoppable. https://punstoppable. com/Stonehenge-puns

Punstoppable. (n.d.). *10 hilarious Alamo puns.* Punstoppable. https://punstoppable. com/alamo-puns

Punstoppable. (n.d.). *11 hilarious Cadillacs puns.* Punstoppable. https://punstoppable. com/cadillacs-puns

Punstoppable. (n.d.). *11 hilarious margarita puns.* Punstoppable. https://punstoppable. com/margarita-puns

Punstoppable. (n.d.). *13 hilarious Wild West puns.* Punstoppable. https:// punstoppable.com/wild-west-puns

Punstoppable. (n.d.). *14 hilarious arbor puns.* Punstoppable. https://punstoppable. com/arbor-puns

Punstoppable. (n.d.). *19 hilarious Robin Hood puns.* Punstoppable. https:// punstoppable.com/robin-hood-puns

Punstoppable. (n.d.). *30 hilarious cabin puns.* Punstoppable. https://punstoppable. com/cabin-puns

Punstoppable. (n.d.). *34 hilarious Elvis puns.* Punstoppable. https://punstoppable. com/elvis-puns

Punstoppable. (n.d.). *34 hilarious ranch puns.* Punstoppable. https://punstoppable. com/ranch-puns

Punstoppable. (n.d.). *40 hilarious Native puns.* Punstoppable. https://punstoppable. com/native-puns

Punstoppable. (n.d.). *42 hilarious junk puns.* Punstoppable. https://punstoppable. com/junk-puns

Punstoppable. (n.d.). *43 hilarious doll puns.* Punstoppable. https://punstoppable. com/doll-puns

Punstoppable. (n.d.). *44 hilarious court puns.* Punstoppable. https://punstoppable.

com/court-puns

Punstoppable. (n.d.). *44 hilarious statues puns.* Punstoppable. https://punstoppable. com/statues-puns

Punstoppable. (n.d.). *45 hilarious performance puns.* Punstoppable. https:// punstoppable.com/Performance-puns

Punstoppable. (n.d.). *46 hilarious sky puns.* Punstoppable. https://punstoppable. com/sky-puns

Punstoppable. (n.d.). *47 hilarious invention puns.* Punstoppable. https://punstoppable. com/Invention-puns

Punstoppable. (n.d.). *47 hilarious tower puns.* Punstoppable. https://punstoppable. com/tower-puns

Rainbow Vomit. (n.d.). *Experiential art gallery in Dallas, TX.* Rainbow Vomit. https:// www.rainbowvomitdallas.com/

RVshare. (2021, May 17). *Top 8 boondocking spots in Texas.* RVshare. https://rvshare. com/blog/boondocking-in-texas/

Scary Mommy. (2019, October 29). *103 classic and hilarious bar jokes that will make you drunk on laughter.* Scary Mommy. https://www.scarymommy.com/bar-jokes/

SeaWorld San Antonio. (2019). *SeaWorld Theme Park - Texas animal attractions.* SeaWorld San Antonio. https://seaworld.com/san-antonio/

Sedgwick County Zoo. (n.d.). *Contact.* Sedgwick County Zoo. https://scz.org/ contact

Sherwood Forest Faire. (n.d.). *Room rentals | Event venue | Austin TX | Bastrop.* Sherwood Forest Faire. https://www.sherwoodforestfaire.com/sherwood- castle-accommodations

Six Flags. (n.d.). *Our rides - Six Flags Over Texas.* Six Flags. https://www.sixflags. com/overtexas/things-to-do/all-rides

Staah. (2019). *20 punniest hotel puns that will have you giggling.* Staah. https://blog. staah.com/tips-trends/20-punniest-hotel-puns-that-will-have-you-giggling

Starlight Theatre Restaurant and Saloon. (n.d.). *The best food and entertainment in the Terlingua Texas Ghost Town.* Starlight Theatre Restaurant and Saloon. http:// www.thestarlighttheatre.com/

Stephanie. (2019, February 27). *50 regal & hilarious castle puns for castle Instagram captions*. History Fangirl. https://historyfangirl.com/jokes-about-castle-puns-for-castle-instagram-captions/

Storm, K. (2020, June 27). *37 timeless Texas quotes + sayings that Texans love*. Lone Star Travel Guide. https://www.lonestartravelguide.com/texas-quotes-caption-ideas/

Taubenfeld, E. (2021, April 3). *50 cow jokes that will make you spit up your milk*. Reader's Digest. https://www.rd.com/article/cow-jokes/

Texas Parks & Wildlife. (2020). *Palo Duro Canyon State Park*. Texas Park and Wildlife. https://tpwd.texas.gov/state-parks/palo-duro-canyon

Texas Parks & Wildlife. (n.d.). *Davis Mountains State Park*. Texas Parks and Wildlife. https://tpwd.texas.gov/state-parks/davis-mountains

Texas Parks & Wildlife Department. (n.d.). *Caddo Lake State Park*. Texas Parks and Wildlife Department. https://tpwd.texas.gov/state-parks/caddo-lake

Texas Parks & Wildlife Department. (n.d.). *Fort Leaton State Historic Site*. Texas Parks & Wildlife Department. https://tpwd.texas.gov/state-parks/fort-leaton

Texas Parks & Wildlife Department. (n.d.). *Indian Lodge*. Texas Parks & Wildlife Department. https://tpwd.texas.gov/state-parks/indian-lodge

Texas Parks & Wildlife Department. (n.d.). *Monahans Sandhills State Park*. Texas Parks & Wildlife Department. https://tpwd.texas.gov/state-parks/monahans-sandhills

The Alamo. (2019, November). *The Alamo*. The Alamo. https://www.thealamo.org/

The Bird Geek. (2021, August 9). *Birdwatching jokes · 27 funny birding jokes and puns*. The Bird Geek. https://thebirdgeek.com/birdwatching-jokes-puns/

The Dad. (2021, January 11). *35+ smokin' hot grilling puns (& jokes) perfect for BBQ season*. The Dad. https://www.thedad.com/grilling-puns-jokes/

The Gage Hotel. (n.d.). *Home*. The Gage Hotel. https://gagehotel.com/

The Menger Bar. (n.d.). *Bars in San Antonio | The historic Menger hotel*. The Menger Bar. https://www.mengerhotel.com/san-antonio-restaurants/menger-bar

Tower of the Americas. (2019, April 12). *Tower of the Americas - Taking entertainment & fine dining to new heights.* Tower of the Americas. https://www. toweroftheamericas.com/

Trahan, K. (n.d.). *Plan your visit.* Exotic Resort Zoo. https://www.zooexotics.com/ plan-your-visit/

Ulrich Museum of Art. (n.d.). *Ulrich Museum of Art.* Ulrich Museum of Art. https://ulrich.wichita.edu/

University of Texas. (n.d.). *Skyspace.* University of Texas. https://turrell.utexas. edu/

Upjoke. (n.d.). *The 10+ best sinkhole jokes.* Upjoke. https://upjoke.com/sinkhole-jokes

Upjoke. (n.d.). *The 16+ best Mentos jokes.* Upjoke. https://upjoke.com/mentos-jokes

Upjoke. (n.d.). *The 24+ best Renaissance jokes.* Upjoke. https://upjoke.com/ renaissance-jokes

Upjoke. (n.d.). *The 38+ best roller coaster jokes.* Upjoke. https://upjoke.com/roller-coaster-jokes

Upjoke. (n.d.). *The 42+ best Rio jokes.* Upjoke. https://upjoke.com/rio-jokes

Upjoke. (n.d.). *The 58+ best aquarium jokes.* Upjoke. https://upjoke.com/aquarium-jokes

Upjoke. (n.d.). *The 74+ best swamp jokes.* Upjoke. https://upjoke.com/swamp-jokes

Upjoke. (n.d.). *The 106+ best museum jokes.* Upjoke. https://upjoke.com/museum-jokes

Upjoke. (n.d.). *The 108+ best cave jokes.* Upjoke. https://upjoke.com/cave-jokes

Upjoke. (n.d.). *The 112+ best sky jokes.* Upjoke. https://upjoke.com/sky-jokes

Wild Berry Farm. (n.d.). *Texas Berry & Flower Farm.* Wild Berry Farm. https:// www.txberry.com/

Wildcatter Ranch. (n.d.). *Texas guest ranch, Texas family reunions, Texas barn wedding venue, corporate retreats, team building, shooting range, horseback riding, archery, tomahawk throwing.* Wildcatter Ranch. https://www.wildcatterranch.com/

Wilkinson, S. (2021, April 21). *50 roar-some lion puns.* Kidadl. https://kidadl.com/ articles/roar-some-lion-puns

Woodrow House Bed and Breakfast. (n.d.). *Woodrow House Bed & Breakfast | Lubbock lodging across from Texas Tech University.* Woodrow House Bed and Breakfast. https://www.woodrowhouse.com/

Worst Jokes Ever. (n.d.). *The 50+ best sky jokes.* Worst Jokes Ever. https://worstjokesever.com/sky

Made in the USA
Coppell, TX
20 July 2023

19408151R00046